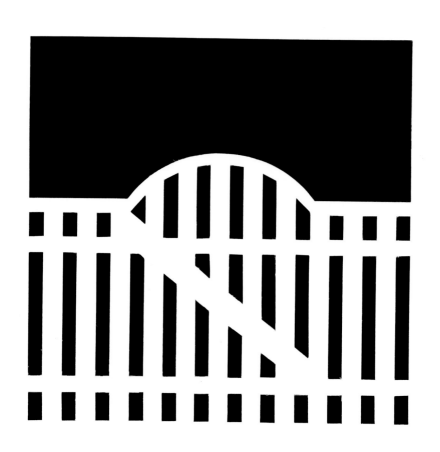

CLAIRE MURRAY
Nantucket Inspirations

Introduction by Claire Murray

Editorial, Design & Photography by Donna Murphy

CMD ENTERPRISES/OSTERVILLE

CMD ENTERPRISES

CLAIRE MURRAY
Nantucket Inspirations

Published in the United States of America by CMD Enterprises
Copyright © 1996 by CMD Enterprises
Osterville, MA

Claire Murray, Nantucket Inspirations
First Edition

Art: Claire Murray
Editorial, Design & Photography: Donna Murphy
Studio Art Production: Anne Beaulieu & David Beaulieu
Computer Art & Production: Martha Flaherty
Chart Formulation: Roberta Q. Cox, Betty Spalt Hall, Margot Conley
Copy Editor: Laurel Kornhiser

ISBN 0-9652613-0-1
Library of Congress Catalog Card Number 96-084868

Printed in the United States of America
by The Hennegan Company, Cincinnati, Ohio

With special thanks

*To three extraordinary women who have
influenced my life's passion and direction:*

*To Jinny Avery for introducing me to quilt making.
To Maggie Meredith for teaching me rug hooking.*

*Special thanks to my mother, Ella Mae, who has given
me strength and encouragement through the years.*

— Claire Murray

CONTENTS

Introduction 6

Mermaids & Myths 12

Landmarks & Legends 42

Seaside Cottages 72

Nantucket Gardens 96

Rug Hooking Instructions 118

Sources & Credits 119

INTRODUCTION

by Claire Murray

I have never regretted

my move from New York to Nantucket. I traded skyscrapers for rose-

covered cottages, the Empire State Building for Sankaty Light, and an

island surrounded by bridges for an island accessible by boat or small

plane. While much of my work today takes me back to New York,

Nantucket is where it all began.

INTRODUCTION

Nantucket's allure is undeniable, at least it was for me. The small, winding cobblestone streets are charming, as are the overflowing window boxes and picket-fenced gardens, found not just in town but throughout the island. What better place to open an inn, I thought. And so I did. The old sea captain's home needed a lot of work, but I knew it would make a perfect destination for summer vacationers, while the tranquility of the winter months would offer me the chance to continue my art career. After months of hard work, Fair Gardens Inn became a home away from home with its trellised gardens and towering rows of foxgloves and hollyhocks.

Shortly after arriving on the island, I was fortunate to meet a woman who would change the course of my life forever. Maggie Meredith soon taught me her method of Nantucket rug hooking. Maggie preferred yarn to the wool strips used by the women who pioneered this art hundreds of years ago. Although the technique was the same, the use of yarn versus wool gave the rug a different look when it was finished. Conveniently, a local needlepoint shop in town offered an endless supply of yarn for all of the rug hookers on the island. Once exposed to this art form, I was hooked.

My surroundings supplied me with infinite inspiration. The wild bunnies that frolicked under the hollyhocks in the garden outside of my art studio inspired *English Garden Runner*, one of my original designs, for which I am perhaps best known. Over the years, many people have commented on my unique sense of color. I have created a palette that relates directly to the hues of Nantucket: the cornflower blue skies, the silver shingles, the white-washed picket fences, the pink cascading roses, and the bright accent colors so prevalent in the seaside gardens for which Nantucket is renowned.

My first book, *Claire Murray, Nantucket Inspirations*, is a collection which I feel captures Nantucket's unique qualities, from her seafaring history to the seaside cottages and gardens that still draw us to her.

ABOUT THIS BOOK

Nantucket Inspirations is divided into four chapters: Mermaids & Myths, Landmarks & Legends, Seaside Cottages, and Nantucket Gardens. Each chapter features several designs with color charts and formulas for needlepointing, cross stitching, and rug hooking. The needlepoint and counted cross stitch designs have been adapted from the original hooked rug, and in some cases are quite similar. You will, however, notice that some of the needlepoint and counted cross stitch designs differ significantly from their hooked rug cousins. This is simply because a hooked rug cannot have the same amount of detail that you will find in many needlepoint projects.

First time rug hookers should refer to our instructions on page 118, and rest assured that once you get the hang of this simple technique, your project will provide endless hours of satisfaction and relaxation. I like to encourage rug hookers to experiment and have fun, as rug hooking is extremely forgiving and is not as exacting and restrictive as needlepoint or counted cross stitch. Once you have chosen your design, you must decide whether to tackle the project from scratch or purchase a prepared kit containing printed jute, hook, and yarn. If you are starting from scratch, we recommend that you purchase jute that measures one foot larger on all sides than the size of the design you have chosen. When purchasing jute, stay away from the inexpensive burlap found in many craft stores. The jute you use should be specifically made for rug hooking. You will then have to trace (similar to a coloring book) the outline of the design and have it enlarged to its actual finished size. Once transferred to the jute, you are ready to begin.

Our rugs are made using the finest 100% 6-ply wool yarn. If you decide to purchase a kit, you will receive the proper quantity needed to complete your rug. But if you are tackling the project on your own, you must choose your yarn according to the rug formulas provided in this book.

ABOUT THIS BOOK

While we have done our best to provide the most accurate amounts of yarn for each project, please be aware that rug hookers use different tension, and therefore rug yarn amounts vary from hooker to hooker, as well as from yarn to yarn. Wool strip rug hookers should use our color palette but calculate their own wool amounts.

This book does not include needlepoint and counted cross stitch instructions and presumes that those taking on these projects have needle art experience. If you are interested in learning how to needlepoint and cross stitch, our kits include detailed instructions as well as all of the materials needed to complete the project. Needlepointers should purchase enough #13 mesh canvas to leave at least three inches outside the border of your needlepoint design. You should also purchase enough yarn of your last color so that you can needlepoint three additional outside rows for finishing your needlepoint pillow. Counted cross stitchers should purchase enough #14 count Aida cloth so that there is at least three inches all around the design to allow for a matted area when framing. Please refer to page 119 for a complete listing of the sources and information that will be helpful to you in beginning your project.

I would also like to point out that we have done our very best to reproduce properly the yarn colors in finished rugs found in this book. We have done the same for the color palettes and charts provided to make each project. But, in fact, our own yarn colors vary slightly with each dye lot. For this reason, I encourage you to buy enough yarn at one time to complete your project.

It has given me a great deal of pleasure to gather some of my favorite Nantucket-inspired designs for this book and to offer these charts and formulas for the first time. It is my hope that these designs will help you to bring the beauty and charm of Nantucket into your homes.

When the fog settles over "The Gray Lady," not even the flashing red and white beacon from Sankaty Light can reach whaling vessels far off shore. The Atlantic has taken many men, even on the best of sailing days, leaving widows to ponder the fate of their loved ones. Perhaps an unexpected squall caught the crew off guard, or perhaps they were lured into unforgiving seas by the siren's song.

Mermaids & Myths

Sirens of the Sea

*L*ow as the dash of summer's sea,

Comes to the ear that melody.

Now louder swells the choral strain,

As nearer comes a white-robed train.

The sirens of the sea are there,

Bright Nereids with their golden hair.

— "Neptune's Palace," T. N. Stone, M.D.

SIRENS OF THE SEA

Hooked Rug Chart

(See page 20 for color palette and formula)

SIRENS OF THE SEA

Sirens of the Sea, designed in 1995, captures alluring sirens in song off the coast of Nantucket with the Island's landmarks prominent along the shore. The hooked rug, which features three mermaids, measures 38" x 60". The needlepoint and counted cross stitch design features one mermaid and measures approximately 14" x 14".

Needlepoint: No. 13 mesh canvas – 18" strands
Counted Cross Stitch: No. 14 light blue Aida cloth with 18" strands split from six to three

	YARN OUNCES	NEEDLEPOINT STRANDS	DMC STRANDS		YARN OUNCES	NEEDLEPOINT STRANDS	DMC STRANDS
White #1	6	48	#B5200 - 18				
Putty #9B	4	14	#524 - 6	Heath Green #88	3/4	10	#988 - 5
Sage #9C	4	20	#522 - 8	Spring Green #88A	1/2	8	#907 - 4
Nutria #9D	4	20	#3011 - 8	Cedar Green #89	2	15	#319 - 7
Primrose Yellow #12	1/4	3	#744 - 2	Hemp Brown #92	2	14	#3820 - 8
Hollyhock #23	1	8	#352 - 3	Ginger #93	1	6	#782 - 3
Scallop Pink #26	1	5	#776 - 3	Sand #94	4	48	#3774 - 18
Field Flower #27	1	5	#3708 - 3	Cork #94A	8	48	#950 -18
Cranberry Pink #28	1/4	1	#891 - 3	Old Pine #95	1	6	#436 - 3
Pomegranate #33C	1/4	5	#720 - 2	Potato Skin #96	1	3	#301 - 2
Heather Pink #34	1	9	#605 - 4	Whaler Brown #99	1	12	#3772 - 6
Wisteria #45	1/4	5	#211 - 2	Oatmeal #102	2	19	#842 - 8
Lupin #49	1/4	2	#340 - 1	Bluefish #107	4	15	#3811 - 7
Blue Smoke #54A	10	50	#775 - 30	Juniper #108	4	15	#991 - 7
Bayberry #58	10	75	Aida Cloth	Gull Gray #110	2	15	#932 - 7
Delphinium #59	8	50	#799 - 20	Shingle Gray #112	1	15	#453 - 7
Mist Blue #62A	4	15	#598 - 7	Rose Ash #113	1	6	#3802 - 3
Whaler Blue #68A	4	15	#992 - 8	Quaker Gray #115	1	2	#414 - 2
Sea Green #86	1	4	#472 - 2	Anchor Gray #117	1	5	#317 - 3
Lichen Green #87	2	8	#3346 - 4	Black #120	1/2	3	#310 - 1

Nantucket Bride

Ten thousand years have passed and gone,
Since first she sat that throne upon, —
Since there, the ocean's king beside,
She blushed a timid, trembling bride.

— *"Neptune's Palace," T.N. Stone, M.D.*

Her golden locks, beneath the crown

In waving ringlets flowing down,

Their sunny beauty grandly show

Upon those shoulders, white as snow.

'Neath arching brows, twin orbs of blue,

Outrivaling the ocean's hue,

Shine with a quiet, witching flame,

Passion to kindle, or to tame;

Where sleep the charms, that faithful hold,

Ten thousand years, the sea king bold.

— "Neptune's Palace," T. N. Stone, M.D.

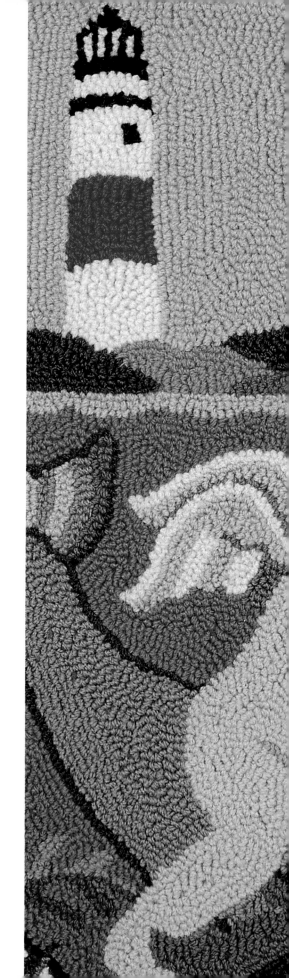

THUS NEPTUNE SPAKE — DISMISSED HIS COURT;

THEY FILLED THE DAY WITH SONG AND SPORT;

THEN EACH RETURNED TO DISTANT HOME

BENEATH THE CRESTED BILLOWS' FOAM.

— *"Neptune's Palace," T.N. Stone, M.D.*

26

NANTUCKET BRIDE

Hooked Rug Chart

(See page 28 for color palette and formula)

NANTUCKET BRIDE

Nantucket Bride, designed in 1995, is a whimsical depiction of a beautiful mermaid bride. The hooked rug measures 34" x 48", while the needlepoint and counted cross stitch design has been squared and measures approximately 14" x 14".

Needlepoint: No. 13 mesh canvas – 18" strands
Counted Cross Stitch: No. 14 medium blue Aida cloth with 18" strands split from six to three

	YARN OUNCES	NEEDLEPOINT STRANDS	DMC STRANDS		YARN OUNCES	NEEDLEPOINT STRANDS	DMC STRANDS
White #1	4	40	#B5200 - 20	Lichen Green #87	3/4	8	#3346 - 4
Mustard Seed #8	1	19	#3821 - 10	Cedar Green #89	1	8	#319 - 4
Putty #9B	3/4	8	#524 - 4	Hawser #91	2	10	#729 - 5
Sage #9C	3/4	8	#522 - 4	Ginger #93	1/4	4	#782 - 3
Nutria #9D	3/4	10	#3011 - 5	Sand #94	4	15	#3774 - 8
Chestnut #21	1/2	8	#400 - 4	Cork #94A	6	30	#950 - 15
Scallop Pink #26	1/4	2	#776 - 1	Coffee #100	1/4	8	#801- 4
Field Flower #27	1/4	1	#3708 - 1	Oatmeal #102	1	7	#842 - 4
Cranberry Pink #28	1/4	X	X	Bluefish #107	2	8	#3811 - 4
Pomegranate #33C	2	X	X	Juniper #108	2	25	#991 - 12
Heather Pink #34	1 1/4	1	#604 - 1	Gull Gray #110	3	36	#932 - 18
Blue Smoke #54A	4	40	#775 - 20	Flagstone #110A	2	36	#931 - 18
Delphinium #59	10	60	Aida Cloth	Shingle Gray #112	6	20	#453 - 10
Mist Blue #62A	2	20	#598 - 10	Rose Ash #113	2	X	X
Whaler Blue #68A	2	20	#992 - 10	Anchor Gray #117	6	50	#317 - 20
Sea Green #86	3/4	8	#472 - 4	Black #120	2	9	#310 - 4

Sea Urchin

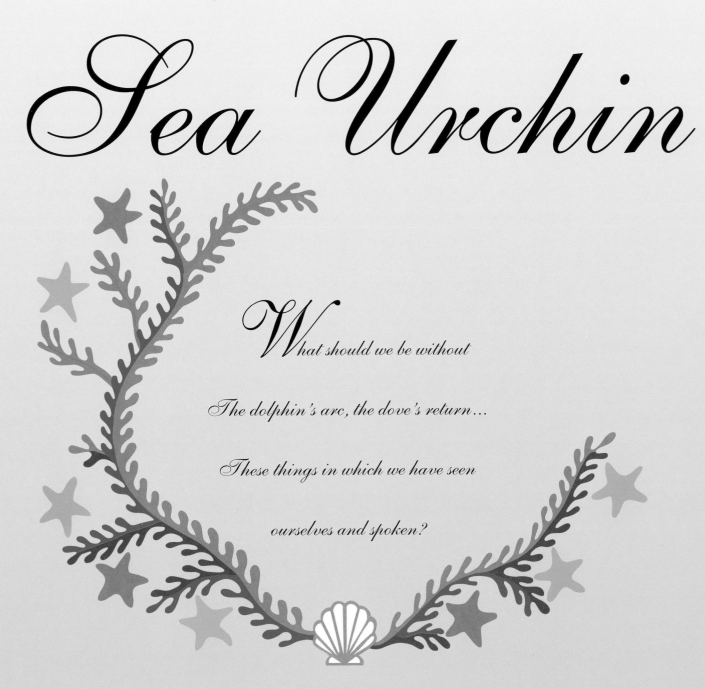

What should we be without

The dolphin's arc, the dove's return…

These things in which we have seen

ourselves and spoken?

— "Advice to a Prophet," Richard Wilbur

SEA URCHIN
Hooked Rug Chart
(See page 35 for color palette & formula)

We shall feel we belong

To the sky and the sea…

— *"The Sand Siren," Joshua Freeman Crowell*

SEA URCHIN

Sea Urchin, designed in 1995, is a companion piece to Sirens of the Sea and
Nantucket Bride. This oval rug with clamshell border measures 24" x 36". The needlepoint and
counted cross stitch version of this design has been squared and measures approximately 14" x 14".

Needlepoint: No. 13 mesh canvas - 18" strands
Counted Cross Stitch: No. 14 medium blue Aida cloth with 18" strands split from six to three

	YARN OUNCES	NEEDLEPOINT STRANDS	DMC STRANDS		YARN OUNCES	NEEDLEPOINT STRANDS	DMC STRANDS
White #1	1 1/2	18	#B5200 - 6				
Putty #9B	1	5	#524 - 2	Lichen Green #87	1	12	#3346 - 5
Sage #9C	1	4	#522 - 3	Cedar Green #89	1	4	#319 - 1
Nutria #9D	1 1/2	10	#3011 - 6	Sand #94	4	15	#3774 - 9
Orange Sherbert #16	3/4	7	#3340 - 4	Cork #94A	1/2	6	#950 - 2
Hollyhock #23	3/4	5	#352 - 3	Old Pine #95	1/2	6	#436 - 2
Scallop Pink #26	1/4	1	#776 - 1	Potato Skin #96	1/2	5	#301 - 2
Field Flower #27	1/4	1	#3708 - 1	Whaler Brown #99	1/4	2	#3772 - 1
Cranberry Pink #28	1/2	2	#891 - 2	Oatmeal #102	1/2	16	#842 - 8
Pomegranate #33C	3/4	4	#720 - 3	Bleached Oak #104	1/2	15	#840 - 8
Bayberry #58	12	100	Aida Cloth	Juniper #108	4	X	X
Mist Blue #62A	4	30	#598 - 14	Shingle Gray #112	5	20	#453 - 10
Whaler Blue #68A	3	X	X	Rose Ash #113	2	10	#3802 - 6
Sea Green #86	1 1/2	18	#472 - 8	Black #120	1/4	3	#310 - 2

When to the sailor, on some placid sea,

Came the low song, of mermaid melody,

Soft as the whispers of the evening breeze,

Strong as the current of the treacherous seas.

— "Neptune's Vow," T. N. Stone, M.D.

Mermaid

The Sea-goddess

My cabinets are oyster-shells,
In which I keep my orient pearls;
To open them I use the tide,
As keys to locks, which opens wide
The oyster shells, then out I take
Those orient pearls and crowns do make;
And modest coral I do wear,
Which blushes when it touches air.
On silver waves I sit and sing,
And then the fish lie listening:
Then sitting on a rocky stone
I comb my hair with fishes' bone;
The whilst Apollo with his beams
Doth dry my hair from watery streams.
His light doth glaze the water's face,
Make the large sea my looking-glass:
So when I swim on waters high,
I see myself as I glide by:
But when the sun begins to burn,
I back into my waters turn,
And dive unto the bottom low:
Then on my head the waters flow
In curlëd waves and circles round,
And thus with waters am I crowned.

Margaret Cavendish
Duchess of Newcastle

MERMAID

Designed in 1988, Mermaid has become one of Claire's most popular and recognized designs. The Mermaid oval hooked rug, done in sea greens and blues, measures 32" x 44". The needlepoint and counted cross stitch version of this design has been squared and slightly adapted to measure approximately 14" x 14".

Needlepoint: No. 13 mesh canvas – 18" strands
Counted Cross Stitch: No. 14 light blue Aida cloth with 18" strands split from six to three

	YARN OUNCES	NEEDLEPOINT STRANDS	DMC STRANDS		YARN OUNCES	NEEDLEPOINT STRANDS	DMC STRANDS
White #1	8	18	#B5200 - 6	Whaler Blue #68A	8	20	#992 - 11
Flesh #21B	4	22	#945 - 13	Celery #86A	2	30	#369 - 14
Peach #22	1	3	#3824 - 3	Spring Green #88A	2	22	#907 - 13
Hollyhock #23	1	4	#352 - 3	Cork #94A	2	6	#950 - 2
Scallop Pink #26	1/2	2	#776 - 2	Old Pine #95	2	15	#436 - 4
Blue Smoke #54A	10	150	Aida Cloth	Oatmeal #102	4	12	#842 - 8
Bayberry #58	8	100	#3325 - 20	Driftwood #103	2	12	#841 - 4
Delphinium #59	2	X	X	Juniper #108	6	28	#991 - 14
Mist Blue #62A	8	30	#598 - 16	Black #120	1/4	3	#310 - 1

Three hundred years of New England weather have not loosened Main Street's cobblestones or the brick mansions that snuggle the town's narrow streets. Nantucket foundations are rich in history and story. Their strength symbolizes islanders who endured long winter months and the dangers of life at sea. Purple and blue hydrangea blooms cascade onto the old brick sidewalks and weathered walkways in this town that time has forgotten.

Landmarks & Legends

Nantucket Village

On uttermost tip of the harbor land,

Buttressed by rock on shelving sand,

Daring the waves' and stormwinds' might,

A pillar by day, and a flame by night,

The little Brant Point Light

— "Brant Point Light," William Wells Jordan

Far out to sea my happy island lies,
With mists and sunlight playing round its shore;
There waves break ever, and the wild gull cries,
And carefree winds are whistling evermore.

Its windswept moors hold wavelike dunes of sand,
Where pine and fern and bay perfume the air,
And in wide spaces by the fragrance fanned,
The burdened spirit loses all its care.

The quaint old town has many a narrow street,
Where houses gray with age and weather be,
And boatlined wharves of sheds where fishers meet,
And over all, the romance of the sea.

Spell of the past lies on the ancient town,
Its whaling fleet once sailed far o'er the world,
And homeward brought the sea's wealth and renown,
Each hailed with joy, as stormbeat sails were furled.

— *William Wells Jordan*

The old town sits and dreams of bygone days,
The island sleeps in peace on ocean's breast,
Far from the mainland's crowded cares and frays,
And there the worldworn toiler findeth rest.

There sweeping sunsets flame o'er moor and sea,
There stars and mystic moonlight fill the night,
There sunlit waters laugh and dance in glee,
The world lies past the sea line out of sight.

That isle's far voice keeps calling unto me
To leave the thronging world, life's rugged fight,
And sail far down blue stretches of the sea,
Where waits in calm the isle of my delight.

NANTUCKET VILLAGE
Hooked Rug Chart

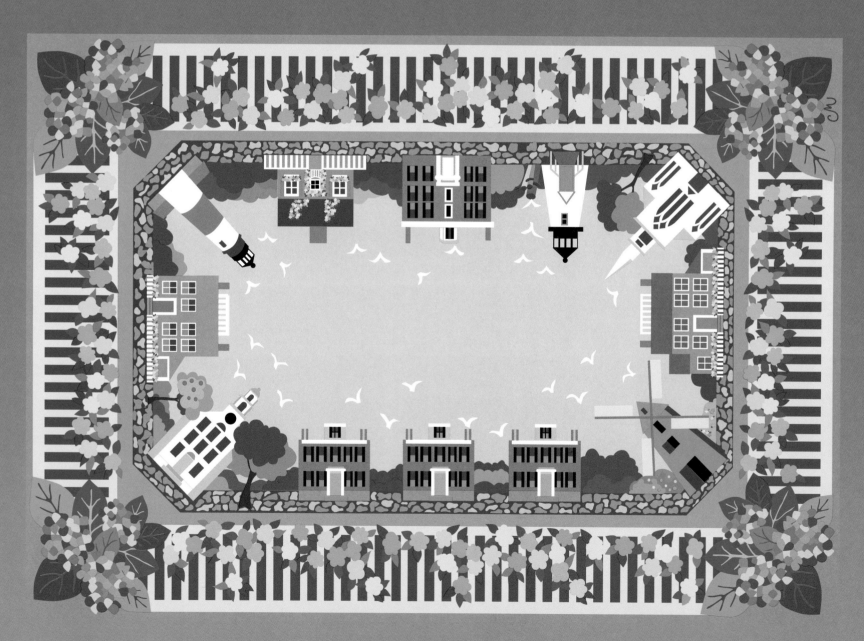

NANTUCKET VILLAGE
Hooked Rug Color Palette and Formula

Nantucket Village, designed in 1992, features Nantucket's landmarks
surrounded by the rose-covered picket fences prevalent throughout the island.
The rug may be hooked in two sizes: with the picket fence border, which measures
53" x 65" or without the picket fence border, which measures 36" x 49".

	YARN OUNCES			YARN OUNCES
White #1	16		Lichen Green #87	6
Whalebone #2	14		White Grape #87A	3
Scallop Pink #26	4		Heath Green #88	3
Cherry Blossom #26A	4		Spring Green #88A	3
Field Flower #27	4		Snap Pea Green #88B	4
Cranberry Pink #28	1		Cedar Green #89	4
Brick Red #33A	1/4		Coffee #100	1
Pomegranate #33C	4		Oatmeal #102	4
Heather Pink #34	4		Bleached Oak #104	2
Lilac #46	2		Juniper #108	12
Lupin #49	2		Gull Gray #110	4
Wild Violet #50	2		Shingle Gray #112	10
Blue Smoke #54A	18		Rose Ash #113	4
Bayberry #58	8		Hull Gray #116	1
Delphinium #59	1		Anchor Gray #117	2
Whaler Blue #68A	2 1/2		Black #120	2

NANTUCKET VILLAGE SAMPLER

Nantucket Village Sampler, designed in 1996, captures
Nantucket's landmarks and charm. Both the needlepoint and
counted cross stitch designs measure approximately 14" x 14".

Needlepoint: No. 13 mesh canvas – 18" strands
Counted Cross Stitch: No. 14 white Aida cloth with 18" strands split from six to three

	NEEDLEPOINT STRANDS	DMC STRANDS		NEEDLEPOINT STRANDS	DMC STRANDS
White #1	25	Aida Cloth	Lichen Green #87	20	#3346 - 10
Whalebone #2	75	Blanc - 20	White Grape #87A	20	#772 - 10
Scallop Pink #26	15	#776 - 7	Heath Green #88	20	#988 - 10
Cherry Blossom #26A	15	#819 - 8	Spring Green #88A	20	#907 - 10
Field Flower #27	15	#3708 - 8	Snap Pea Green #88B	20	#937 - 10
Cranberry Pink #28	19	#891 - 9	Cedar Green #89	40	#319 - 20
Brick Red #33A	3	#347 - 2	Coffee #100	10	#801 - 5
Pomegranate #33C	14	#720 - 6	Oatmeal #102	12	#842 - 6
Heather Pink #34	15	#605 - 8	Bleached Oak #104	20	#840 - 10
Lilac #46	15	#210 - 8	Juniper #108	40	#991 - 20
Lupin #49	15	#340 - 8	Gull Gray #110	7	#932 - 4
Wild Violet #50	15	#3746 - 7	Shingle Gray #112	50	#453 - 23
Blue Smoke #54A	45	#775 - 20	Rose Ash #113	10	#3802 - 2
Bayberry #58	45	#3325 - 20	Hull Gray #116	4	#414 - 2
Delphinium #59	20	#799 - 10	Anchor Gray #117	10	#317 - 5
Whaler Blue #68A	15	#992 - 7	Black #120	6	#310 - 3

Oh, the rare old Whale, mid storm and gale

In his ocean home will be,

A giant in might, where might is right,

And King of the boundless sea!

—*Nantucket Whale Song*
(author unknown)

Nantucket Sleighride

A Nantucket Sleighride

"A harpooned whale will usually 'sound' at once, often going down

very deep and remaining under for the better part of an hour. On

rising to the surface, he will often 'run,' that is, swim away at high

speed, dragging the boat after him by the whale line. From time

immemorial this method of marine travel has been known as a

'Nantucket sleigh ride' and a very exciting trip it can be."

– *The Nantucket Scrap Basket*, William F. Macy

NANTUCKET SLEIGHRIDE

Hooked Rug Chart

(See page 58 for color palette and formula)

Whaler Pluck

A whaler from Nantucket town
He had the worst o' luck;
He sailed far off around Cape Horn,
But not a whale he struck.

Three years he cruised, North, South, East, West —
From pole to torrid zone;
But when he laid his course for home
He'd neither oil nor bone.

Yet as he sailed around Brant Point
He set his pennant high,
And when he tied up at the wharf
He lustily did cry:

'We've come home "clean" as we went out
We didn't raise a whale;
And we hain't got a bar'l o' ile,
But we had a _damn fine sail!_'

— Gustav Kobbé

NANTUCKET SLEIGHRIDE

*Nantucket Sleighride, designed in 1987, is a whimsical portrayal
of Nantucket's whaling days and the rides that whalers sometimes took after
harpooning a whale. The hooked rug measures 26" x 36", while the needlepoint and
counted cross stitch version has been squared and measures 14" x 14".*

Needlepoint: No. 13 mesh canvas – 18" strands
Counted Cross Stitch: No. 14 light blue Aida cloth with 18" strands split from six to three

	YARN OUNCES	NEEDLEPOINT STRANDS	DMC STRANDS		YARN OUNCES	NEEDLEPOINT STRANDS	DMC STRANDS
White #1	2	12	#B5200 - 9				
Whalebone #2	2 1/2	32	Blanc - 18	Potato Skin #96	1/4	4	#301 - 2
Primrose Yellow #12	1/4	1	#744 -1	Oatmeal #102	1	9	#842 - 4
Flesh #21B	1/2	6	#945 - 1	Bleached Oak #104	6	50	#840 - 30
Brick Red #33A	2	14	#347 - 6	Bluefish #107	1/4	9	#3811 - 4
Lapis #52A	2	53	#336 - 22	Juniper #108	1/4	2	#991 - 1
Blue Smoke #54A	14	125	#775 - 3	Gull Gray #110	5	38	#932 - 18
Cadet Blue #61A	10	66	#826 - 37	Shingle Gray #112	3/4	8	#453 - 3
Whaler Blue #68A	1/4	7	#992 - 3	Rose Ash #113	3/4	14	#3802 - 7
Cork #94A	1/2	12	#950 - 6	Hull Gray #116	3/4	4	#414 - 7
Old Pine #95	1 1/2	5	#436 - 3	Black #120	2	7	#310 - 2

Sankaty Light

YEARS SWEEP ON, AND TIDES SWIRL NIGH,

WHILE COUNTLESS SHIPS GO SAILING BY:

WHERE HUMAN CURRENTS FLOW OUT AND IN,

WHERE VOYAGES END, AND VOYAGES BEGIN.

—"Brant Point Light," William Wells Jordan

Never a Captain grizzled and gray

Now climbs to the house-top walk,

Pipe and spyglass are put away:

But the wise ones sometimes talk

Of the pleasant ghosts that are peering still

Through the glasses out to sea,

Thinking back to the lure of the ships

And the life that used to be.

— "The Walk," Mary Starbuck

SANKATY LIGHT

SANKATY LIGHT

Sankaty Light, designed in 1990, captures Old Ironsides
off the coast of Nantucket. The finished rug measures 30" x 45", while the
needlepoint and counted cross stitch design measures 10" x 14".

Needlepoint: No. 13 mesh canvas - 18" strands
Counted Cross Stitch: No. 14 light blue Aida cloth with 18" strands split from six to three

	YARN OUNCES	NEEDLEPOINT STRANDS	DMC STRANDS		YARN OUNCES	NEEDLEPOINT STRANDS	DMC STRANDS
White #1	2	18	#B5200 - 9				
Whalebone #2	6	30	Blanc - 18	Bisque #91B	1/4	36	#677 - 20
Nutria #9D	1 1/2	15	#3011 - 7	Potato Skin #96	6	40	#301 - 30
Cranberry Pink #28	1/2	8	#891 - 4	Oatmeal #102	5	48	#842 - 14
Brick Red #33A	1/4	3	#347 - 2	Driftwood #103	1	10	#841 - 5
Lapis #52A	1/4	3	#336 - 2	Bluefish #107	1 3/4	3	#3811 - 2
Blue Smoke #54A	8	50	Aida Cloth	Juniper #108	5	20	#991 - 10
Cadet Blue #61A	3 1/2	25	#826 - 14	Shingle Gray #112	2	10	#453 - 5
Mist Blue #62A	3	20	#598 - 10	Rose Ash #113	5	25	#3802 - 14
Whaler Blue #68A	4	20	#992 - 10	Elm Bark #114	2 1/2	15	#300 - 8
Shutter Green #81	1/2	3	#890 - 2	Anchor Gray #117	1	20	#317 - 10
Hawser #91	6	35	#729 - 15	Black #120	18	35	#310 - 12

"I WAS MADE
ON NANTUCKET ISLAND
I AM STRONG AND STOUT
DON'T LOSE OR BURN ME
I'LL NEVER WEAR OUT"

Nantucket Basket

Nantucket

Lightship Baskets

NANTUCKET BASKET

Nantucket Basket was inspired by the original woven baskets made by sailors stationed on Nantucket lightships. The hooked rug, designed in 1987, shows a traditional Nantucket Basket overflowing with island roses. The hooked rug measures 25" x 31". The same design in needlepoint and counted cross stitch measures 12" x 14".

Needlepoint: No. 13 mesh canvas - 18" strands
Counted Cross Stitch: No. 14 white Aida cloth with 18" strands split from six to three

	YARN OUNCES	NEEDLEPOINT STRANDS	DMC STRANDS		YARN OUNCES	NEEDLEPOINT STRANDS	DMC STRANDS
White #1	18	2	#B5200 - 4	Bayberry #58	3	30	#3325 - 5
Primrose Yellow #12	1/2	5	#744 - 2	Cadet Blue #61A	3	30	#826 - 3
Peach #22	1	14	#3824 - 8	Whaler Blue #68A	1	18	#992 - 4
Shrimp #22A	1	7	#353 - 4	Lichen Green #87	3/4	17	#3346 - 5
Hollyhock #23	1	20	#352 - 9	Spring Green #88A	1/2	12	#907 - 5
Scallop Pink #26	2	18	#776 - 3	Cedar Green #89	1/2	15	#319 - 1
Field Flower #27	1	15	#3708 - 4	Hawser #91	2	25	#729 - 11
Cranberry Pink #28	1	8	#891 - 7	Ginger #93	1	20	#782 - 7
Rambler Rose #35	2	12	#957 - 6	Potato Skin #96	1	7	#301 - 3
Blue Smoke #54A	4	30	#775 - 1	Juniper #108	1	12	#991 - 7

NANTUCKET BASKET

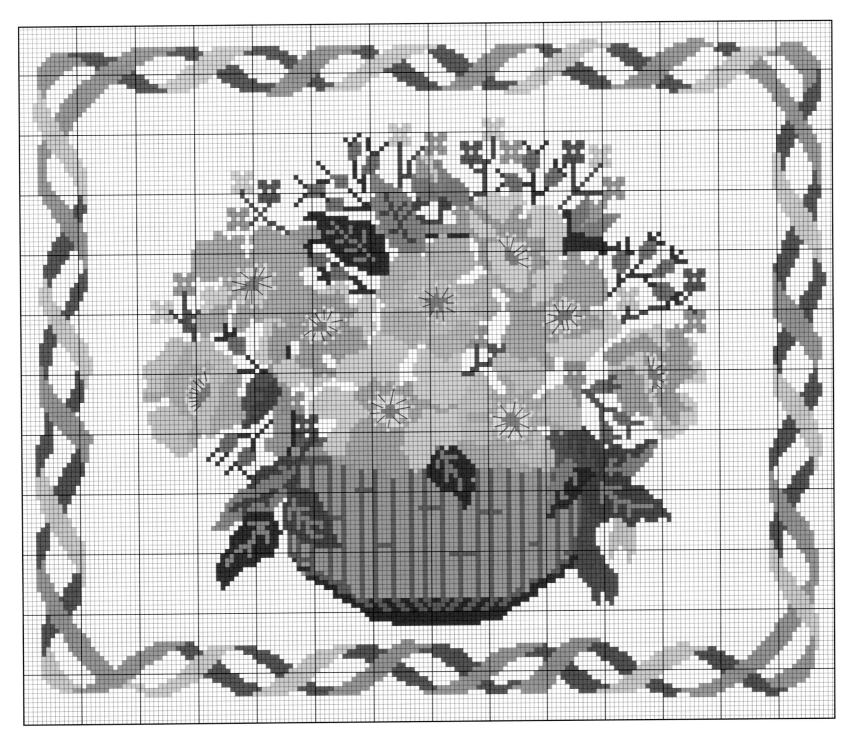

O

verlooking the Atlantic, in an old fishing village a few miles outside of

town, the weathered gray cottages of Siasconset sit side by side on the

bluff. There are a few roads for cars, but the best way to travel is on foot

between the narrow passages created by the tall hedges and picket fences

of each cottage. Foxgloves and hollyhocks grow abundantly by the sea,

as do the geraniums that overflow weathered window boxes. Cottage

rooftops become vibrant blankets of cascading roses in the heat of the

mid-summer sun.

Seaside Cottages

"Small houses on little lanes,

picket fences,  and spicy gardens

that trotted up clamshell walks.

Patches big as pocket handkerchiefs.

 And one patch could hold

all the nice things of life —

a little white cottage, a garden, a wife..."

—An Island Patchwork, Eleanor Early

Home Sweet Home

HOME SWEET HOME

My home is by the sounding sea;

Where billows bound and sport in glee,

Where white-capped waves are crested high

When tempests beat and storms are nigh.

The lights upon the shining beach,

Far out at sea, they glimmering reach,

And guide and cheer the sailor on,

To distant lands or nearer bourne.

— "My Home," L. Eugene Eldridge

HOME SWEET HOME
Hooked Rug Chart

HOME SWEET HOME

Hooked Rug Color Palette and Formula

*Inspired by Nantucket's welcoming seaside cottages,
the Home Sweet Home hooked rug was designed in 1995. The checkered
border of this horizontal rug, which measures 28" x 38", frames
an island cottage surrounded by morning glories and bleeding hearts.*

	YARN OUNCES
White #1	4
Primrose Yellow #12	1/4
Flesh #21B	1/2
Peach #22	1/2
Shrimp #22A	1/2
Hollyhock #23	1/2
Scallop Pink #26	1 1/2
Field Flower #27	1 1/2
Cranberry Pink #28	1/4
Begonia Pink #30	1
Pomegranate #33C	1/2
Heather Pink #34	1/2
Blue Smoke #54A	6
Bayberry #58	2
Delphinium #59	2
Cadet Blue #61A	1/2

	YARN OUNCES
Whaler Blue #68A	3/4
Sea Green #86	3/4
Lichen Green #87	1/2
White Grape #87A	2
Spring Green #88A	1/2
Snap Pea Green #88B	1/2
Cedar Green #89	1/2
Old Pine #95	1/2
Potato Skin #96	1/4
Oatmeal #102	3
Juniper #108	3
Gull Gray #110	2
Shingle Gray #112	6
Rose Ash #113	1
Hull Gray #116	1/4
Black #120	4

HOME SWEET HOME
Needlepoint & Counted Cross Stitch
Color Palette & Formula

The needlepoint and counted cross stitch version of Home Sweet Home was also designed in 1995, but does not include the checkered border of the hooked rug.

Needlepoint: No. 13 mesh canvas - 18" strands
Counted Cross Stitch: No. 14 light blue Aida cloth with 18" strands split from six to three

	NEEDLEPOINT STRANDS	DMC STRANDS		NEEDLEPOINT STRANDS	DMC STRANDS
White #1	30	#B5200 - 15	Whaler Blue #68A	18	#992 - 9
Primrose Yellow #12	3	#744 - 2	Sea Green #86	10	#472 - 5
Flesh #21B	6	#945 - 3	Lichen Green #87	10	#3346 - 5
Peach #22	6	#3824 - 3	White Grape #87A	25	#772 - 15
Shrimp #22A	6	#353 - 3	Spring Green #88A	8	#907 - 4
Hollyhock #23	6	#352 - 3	Snap Pea Green #88B	6	#937 - 4
Scallop Pink #26	11	#776 - 6	Cedar Green #89	10	#319 - 5
Field Flower #27	22	#3708 - 12	Old Pine #95	10	#436 - 5
Cranberry Pink #28	3	#891 - 3	Potato Skin #96	4	#301 - 2
Begonia Pink #30	16	#893 - 8	Oatmeal #102	2	#842 - 1
Pomegranate #33C	8	#720 - 4	Juniper #108	25	#991 - 13
Heather Pink #34	14	#605 - 8	Gull Gray #110	20	#932 - 10
Blue Smoke #54A	16	Aida Cloth	Shingle Gray #112	25	#453 - 15
Bayberry #58	16	#3325 - 10	Rose Ash #113	15	#3802 - 7
Delphinium #59	18	#799 - 9	Hull Gray #116	3	#414 - 2
Cadet Blue #61A	12	#826 - 7	Black #120	30	#310 - 18

Nantucket
Cottages

"Some of the streets in 'Sconset
are only thirty feet long.
And the lanes just wide enough
to trundle a wheelbarrow through.
But honeysuckle burgeons down Broadway,
and ramblers ramp on the roofs."

— An Island Patchwork, Eleanor Early

NANTUCKET COTTAGES

Hooked Rug Chart

(See page 89 for color palette and formula)

NANTUCKET COTTAGES

The Nantucket Cottages hooked rug collection was designed in 1992, while the needlepoint and counted cross stitch version of Nantucket Cottages was designed in 1995. This hooked rug design features six Nantucket cottages and measures 36" x 50" (23" x 36" with two cottages also available). The needlepoint and counted cross stitch design features four cottages and measures approximately 14" x 14".

Needlepoint: No. 13 mesh canvas - 18" strands
Counted Cross Stitch: No. 14 white Aida cloth with 18" strands split from six to three

	YARN OUNCES	NEEDLEPOINT STRANDS	DMC STRANDS
White #1	24	100	Aida Cloth
Primrose #12	1/2	2	#744 - 1
Peach #22	1/4	4	#3824 - 2
Shrimp #22A	1/2	4	#353 - 2
Hollyhock #23	1/2	5	#352 - 3
Scallop Pink #26	2	4	#776 - 2
Field Flower #27	1 1/2	14	#3708 - 6
Cranberry Pink #28	1 1/2	12	#891 - 6
Brick Red #33A	1/4	4	#347 - 2
Pomegranate #33C	2	8	#720 - 4
Heather Pink #34	2	10	#605 - 5
Blue Smoke #54A	4	12	#775 - 6
Bayberry #58	4	10	#3325 - 5
Delphinium #59	4	14	#799 - 6
Cadet Blue #61A	1/4	5	#826 - 3

	YARN OUNCES	NEEDLEPOINT STRANDS	DMC STRANDS
Whaler Blue #68A	8	40	#992 - 18
Lichen Green #87	1	6	#3346 - 3
White Grape #87A	1 1/2	3	#772 - 2
Spring Green #88A	1	8	#907 - 4
Snap Pea Green #88B	6	10	#937 - 5
Old Pine #95	1/2	3	#436 - 2
Oatmeal #102	1 1/2	10	#842 - 5
Bleached Oak #104	1	1	#840 - 1
Juniper #108	4	15	#991 - 7
Gull Gray #110	2	15	#932 - 7
Flagstone #110A	1	7	#931 - 3
Shingle Gray #112	3	20	#453 - 10
Rose Ash #113	3	12	#3802 - 6
Quaker Gray #115	3	6	#414 - 3
Anchor Gray #117	4	6	#317 - 3

Sea breezes are good...

"On the road to Polpis is a little gray house,
smothered in roses like a bride in tulle.
In front of the house is a wee picket fence where
ten thousand pink roses bloom with the honeysuckle.
And in back of the fence is a tiny walk
bordered with sweet alyssum and purple petunias...

I do not know who lives in the little house,
but I hope it is somebody romantic,
because once I passed there in the moonlight,
and the roses were kissing one another..."

—An Island Patchwork, Eleanor Early

...for flowers

Rose cottage

Roses

"The climbing roses of 'Sconset
are joyful sisters who could never say no to a bee.
They are astoundingly prolific and
wantonly cheerful — but not a pure type!
Roses that bloom on an island
have remarkable staying powers.
And in 'Sconset they bloom passionately all summer,
and encourage the bees till they die."

—An Island Patchwork, Eleanor Early

ROSE COTTAGE

Claire's Nantucket art studio, with its rose-covered rooftop, was the inspiration for
Rose Cottage. The hooked rug was designed in 1989 and has been identically adapted
for needlepoint and counted cross stitch. The finished hooked rug measures 27" x 36".
The needlepoint and counted cross stitch design measures 12" x 14".

Needlepoint: No. 13 mesh canvas - 18" strands
Counted Cross Stitch: No. 14 light blue Aida cloth with 18" strands split from six to three

	YARN OUNCES	NEEDLEPOINT STRANDS	DMC STRANDS		YARN OUNCES	NEEDLEPOINT STRANDS	DMC STRANDS
White #1	1	13	#B5200 - 9				
Whalebone #2	2	9	Blanc - 4	Celery #86A	3	26	#369 - 15
Flesh #21B	1 1/4	10	#945 - 7	Lichen Green #87	1 1/2	18	#3346 - 8
Peach #22	2	21	#3824 - 22	Spring Green #88A	4	30	#907 - 15
Hollyhock #23	1	7	#352 - 3	Cedar Green #89	2	11	#319 - 7
Scallop Pink #26	4	28	#776 - 13	Cork #94A	1/4	5	#950 - 6
Field Flower #27	1 1/2	12	#3708 - 7	Old Pine #95	1/2	4	#436 - 6
Cranberry Pink #28	2	12	#891 - 7	Potato Skin #96	1/4	2	#301 - 1
Pomegranate #33C	2	17	#720 - 10	Oatmeal #102	1/2	4	#842 - 7
Heather Pink #34	4	18	#605 - 18	Juniper #108	2	17	#991 - 14
Bayberry #58	7	48	#3325 - 4	Gull Gray #110	3	10	#932 - 2
Cadet Blue #61A	3/4	6	#826 - 2	Shingle Gray #112	1/2	10	#453 - 5
Whaler Blue #68A	2	24	#992 - 6	Rose Ash #113	1 1/2	5	#3802 - 3
Cypress #80	1	14	#895 - 5	Anchor Gray #117	2	36	#317 - 10
Sea Green #86	1/2	7	#472 - 3	Black #120	8	39	#310 - 38

ROSE COTTAGE

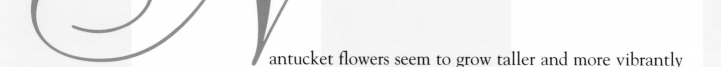

antucket flowers seem to grow taller and more vibrantly

than flowers on the mainland. The pink and coral hollyhocks tower over

the sweet alyssum that crowds the garden path. Bees and butterflies

swarm the summer blooms that lift and turn their heads toward the

afternoon sun. The ocean breeze refreshes the hollyhocks and carries

their fragrance through the garden. Sea breezes are good for flowers.

Nantucket Gardens

The world's a garden;
Pleasures are the flowers...

– "The Garden," Josuah Sylvester

Springtime Fantasy

IN MY GARDEN IN THE MORNING,

WHEN THE BIRDS ARE ON THE WING,

THOUGHTS WITH PEACE AND PLENTY LADEN,

MESSAGES SO CHEERING BRING; –

"WINTER CANNOT CHANGE THE PROSPECT;

ALWAYS JOY WILL FOLLOW STRIFE!"

SO MY GARDEN IN THE MORNING,

SINGS TO ME THE SONG OF LIFE!"

– *"Messages From My Garden," Joshua Freeman Crowell*

SPRINGTIME FANTASY

*The Springtime Fantasy hooked rug collection was designed in 1993, while the
needlepoint and counted cross stitch version was designed in 1996. The rug, which measures 7' x 9',
is too large a hooked rug project, even for the most ambitious. The cottage details of Springtime Fantasy
have been adapted into 14" x 14" needlepoint and counted cross stitch projects.*

Needlepoint: No. 13 mesh canvas - 18" strands
Counted Cross Stitch: No. 14 light blue Aida cloth - 18" strands split from six to three

	NEEDLEPOINT STRANDS	DMC STRANDS		NEEDLEPOINT STRANDS	DMC STRANDS
White #1	18	#B5200 - 9			
Flesh #21B	30	#945 - 15	Lichen Green #87	8	#3346 - 4
Peach #22	15	#3824 - 7	White Grape #87A	8	#772 - 4
Shrimp #22A	15	#353 - 7	Heath Green #88	8	#988 - 4
Hollyhock #23	15	#352 - 8	Spring Green #88A	8	#907 - 4
Scallop Pink #26	26	#776 - 13	Snap Pea Green #88B	15	#937 - 5
Cherry Blossom #26A	10	#819 - 6	Cedar Green #89	10	#319 - 5
Field Flower #27	20	#3708 - 10	Sand #94	6	#3774 - 3
Cranberry Pink #28	8	#891 - 4	Cork #94A	5	#950 - 3
Pomegranate #33C	12	#720 - 6	Old Pine #95	8	#436 - 4
Blue Smoke #54A	3	#775 - 2	Oatmeal #102	4	#842 - 2
Bayberry #58	60	Aida Cloth	Bleached Oak #104	12	#840 - 6
Delphinium #59	2	#799 - 1	Juniper #108	19	#991 - 11
Cadet Blue #61A	4	#826 - 2	Flagstone #110	25	#931 - 12
Mist Blue #62A	50	#598 - 25	Shingle Gray #112	30	#453 - 15
Whaler Blue #68A	60	#992 - 30	Rose Ash #113	9	#3802 - 5

Lattice Garden

Close to the gates a spacious garden lies,

From storms defended, and inclement skies:

Four acres was th' allotted space of ground,

Fenced with a green enclosure all around.

- from Homer's Odyssey, Book VII, Alexander Pope

QUEEN ROSE OF THE ROSEBUD GARDEN OF GIRLS,

COME HITHER, THE DANCES ARE DONE,

IN GLOSS OF SATIN AND GLIMMER OF PEARLS,

QUEEN LILY AND ROSE IN ONE;

SHINE OUT, LITTLE HEAD, SUNNING OVER WITH CURLS,

TO THE FLOWERS, AND BE THEIR SUN.

– FROM "MAUD," ALFRED, LORD TENNYSON

LATTICE GARDEN

LATTICE GARDEN

*Lattice Garden, designed in 1990, features two Nantucket bunnies
spotted in a rose-covered lattice garden. The finished rug measures 31" x 38", while the
needlepoint and counted cross stitch version measures approximately 13" x 14".*

Needlepoint: No. 13 mesh canvas - 18" strands
Counted Cross Stitch: No. 14 white Aida cloth with 18" strands split from six to three

	YARN OUNCES	NEEDLEPOINT STRANDS	DMC STRANDS		YARN OUNCES	NEEDLEPOINT STRANDS	DMC STRANDS
White #1	14	80	Aida Cloth				
Primrose Yellow #12	1/2	3	#744 - 2	Whaler Blue #68A	3	12	#992 - 7
Flesh #21B	1	6	#945 - 3	Cypress #80	1	3	#895 - 2
Peach #22	1	5	#3824 - 3	Sea Green #86	2	5	#472 - 3
Shrimp #22A	1	5	#353 - 3	Celery #86A	1/2	5	#369 - 3
Hollyhock #23	1	5	#352 - 3	Lichen Green #87	2	8	#3346 - 4
Scallop Pink #26	2	12	#776 - 6	Heath Green #88	1/2	4	#998 - 2
Cherry Blossom #26A	1	12	#819 - 6	Spring Green #88A	1 1/2	6	#907 - 3
Field Flower #27	3	12	#3708 - 6	Cedar Green #89	2	18	#319 - 7
Cranberry Pink #28	1/2	2	#891 - 1	Cork #94A	1/2	5	#950 - 3
American Beauty #31	1/2	3	#3705 - 2	Old Pine #95	1/2	2	#436 - 1
Pomegranate #33C	1/4	3	#720 - 1	Potato Skin #96	1	3	#301 - 2
Heather Pink #34	3	16	#605 - 7	Oatmeal #102	2	6	#842 - 3
Blue Smoke #54A	1/2	10	#775 - 5	Juniper #108	10	30	#991 - 15
Bayberry #58	1/2	3	#3325 - 2	Shingle Gray #112	1	5	#453 - 3
Delphinium #59	1/2	1	#799 - 1	Black #120	8	30	#310 - 15

English Garden Runner

One summer day,
I chanced to stray
To a garden of flowers blooming wild.
It took me once more
To the dear days of yore
And a spot that I loved as a child

There were the phlox,
Tall hollyhocks,
Violets perfuming the air,
Frail eglantines,
Shy columbines,
And marigolds everywhere...

— "An Old-Fashioned Garden," Cole Porter

Here, in this sequestered close,

Bloom the hyacinth and rose;

Here beside the modest stock

Flaunts the flaring hollyhock;

Here, without a pang, one sees

Ranks, conditions, and degrees.

– "A Garden Song,"
Henry Austin Dobson

ENGLISH GARDEN RUNNER

Designed in 1989, English Garden Runner has become one of
Claire's most popular designs, and the design for which she is best known. The wild rabbits
that frolicked in the gardens outside her Nantucket art studio inspired this runner, which measures
24" x 64". Foxgloves and hollyhocks provide a dramatic background for the playful bunnies.

YARN OUNCES		YARN OUNCES	
White #1	14		
Primrose Yellow #12	1	Whaler Blue #68A	6
Flesh #21B	1	Cypress #80	2
Peach #22	1	Sea Green #86	2
Shrimp #22A	1	Lichen Green #87	4
Hollyhock #23	1	White Grape #87A	2
Scallop Pink #26	2	Heath Green #88	2
Cherry Blossom #26A	1	Spring Green #88A	2
Cranberry Pink #28	1	Cedar Green #89	2
Heather #34	3	Cork #94A	1
Dusty Rose #34A	1	Potato Skin #96	1
Vin Rose #34B	2	Oatmeal #102	1
Claret #34C	2	Driftwood #103	1
Rambler Rose #35	1	Juniper #108	8
Blue Smoke #54A	1	Shingle Gray #112	2
Bayberry #58	1	Rose Ash #113	1
Delphinium #59	1	Black #120	14

ENGLISH GARDEN

English Garden Runner's needlepoint and counted cross stitch companion was designed in 1991. Although the design has been squared, and measures 14" x 14", it still features the same three bunnies playing underneath Nantucket foxgloves and hollyhocks.

Needlepoint: No. 13 mesh canvas - 18" strands
Counted Cross Stitch: No. 14 black Aida cloth with 18" strands split from six to three

	NEEDLEPOINT STRANDS	DMC STRANDS		NEEDLEPOINT STRANDS	DMC STRANDS
White #1	100	#B5200 - 20			
Primrose Yellow #12	2	#744 - 1	Whaler Blue #68A	35	#992 - 18
Flesh #21B	3	#945 - 2	Cypress #80	18	#895 - 9
Peach #22	5	#3824 - 3	Sea Green #86	23	#472 - 12
Shrimp #22A	3	#353 - 2	Lichen Green #87	26	#3346 - 13
Hollyhock #23	6	#352 - 3	White Grape #87A	23	#772 - 12
Scallop Pink #26	10	#776 - 5	Heath Green #88	15	#998 - 8
Cherry Blossom #26A	6	#819 - 3	Spring Green #88A	13	#907 - 9
Cranberry Pink #28	5	#891 - 3	Cedar Green #89	13	#319 - 8
Heather #34	14	#605 - 7	Cork #94A	3	#950 - 2
Dusty Rose #34A	5	#604 - 3	Potato Skin #96	3	#301 - 2
Vin Rose #34B	5	#3689 - 3	Oatmeal #102	12	#842 - 6
Claret #34C	5	#3688 - 3	Driftwood #103	12	#841 - 6
Rambler Rose #35	5	#957 - 2	Juniper #108	50	#991 - 18
Blue Smoke #54A	4	#775 - 2	Shingle Gray #112	10	#453 - 5
Bayberry #58	2	#3325 - 1	Rose Ash #113	4	#3802 - 2
Delphinium #59	4	#799 - 2	Black #120	90	Aida Cloth

RUG HOOKING INSTRUCTIONS

To begin your project: You must first trace the design you have chosen, enlarge the design to its finished size, and then transfer it onto your jute. If you are using yarn rather than wool strips, roll your yarn into balls. Make a color chart by punching holes one inch apart on a piece of cardboard. Cut and tie a three inch piece of yarn for every color used in your rug project, and mark the color number in pen.

It is very important to select a comfortable chair. Make sure that your feet touch the floor, although some rug hookers are more comfortable using a reclining chair with their feet elevated. Create a rug frame with your lap. You may also use a frame, but it is not necessary. The ball of yarn should be on the floor with the yarn strand reaching to your lap. Tuck the rug jute under your upper legs keeping the jute taut as though it is on a frame. Keep the section you are hooking positioned in the middle of your lap.

Step 1: With the rug jute on your lap, place your left hand (if you are left-handed, place your right hand) under the jute. Your left hand will feed the hook and keep tension as you pull the yarn through with your right hand.

Step 2: Insert the hook into the jute and with a slight twist retrieve the strand of yarn, which your left hand is holding. Pull the yarn up through the jute trying not to split the yarn. It is best to start with a color in the center leaving a two inch tail.

Step 3: Place the yarn around the hook, holding the loop with your fingers. Leave an inch of slack yarn between your jute and the loop you are picking up to prevent pulling out your previous stitch. Draw the loop up through your jute, pulling up gently until your loop stops. You can feel the tension as it tightens against your previous stitch. This will produce a smooth stitch on the back of your work. Adjust the loop height to leave a quarter inch loop on the surface of your work. Hook inside the line of an individual shape, leaving the printed lines as spaces between colors. Continue with this process until the color you are working with is completely filled in.

Step 4: When the shape you are hooking is filled in with color, bring your last loop up approximately one half inch higher than your regular pile. Clip the loop in the center, leaving a tail. It is best to leave the tails on your rug until you are done hooking that area. Then go back and clip tails even with surface.

Binding: While there are many ways to bind your rug, this method is the most popular with our hookers. Use cording that is approximately 1/4" to 3/8" in width and as long as the perimeter of your rug. Place cording on the underside next to the edge of the rug. Wrap the jute around the cording, which will be overcast with the same color as the edge of the rug. Completely cover the jute all the way around so the finished rug will look like it has a corded edge. Miter the corners. It will be a bit bulky, but it will lie flat in the end. When this is done, hand sew the binding as close to the cording as possible. Then trim the jute so the binding will hide the jute edge. Hand sew the other side of the binding to finish.

Helpful Hints: We recommend that you bring the loops up one inch then down to the 1/4" height. You know the yarn has not been split if it comes up easily through the canvas. Sometimes it helps to wiggle the hook through the canvas in tight areas. As you become accustomed to hooking, you will find your loops will become more consistent in height.

Do not cross yarns on the back side. Crossed threads can cause the rug to snag and will create a lump that will be discernible when the rug is on the floor. In order for your rug to be soft and pliable, you should see canvas between the rows of yarn on the reverse side of your rug.

Everyone develops his or her own method of hooking and holding their hook. Try different ways, see what works best for you, and have fun!

SOURCES AND SUPPLIES

Hooked Rug Kits: You may order a complete kit for all of the designs shown in this book. Each kit includes printed jute with the design of your choice, 100% wool yarn, hook, and detailed rug hooking instructions. If you decide to purchase your own yarn, you may order only the printed jute with the Claire Murray design you have chosen.

Needlepoint & Counted Cross Stitch Kits: Complete kits are available for all of the designs in this book. Needlepoint kits include printed canvas, yarn, and needlepointing instructions. Counted cross stitch kits include chart, DMC, and counted cross stitching instructions.

Claire Murray Yarns: Claire's yarns are made out of the finest 100% wool and dyed to her unique color palette. If you purchase your own yarn or use wool strips, we cannot guarantee that the formulas provided will be adequate, as they are based on Claire Murray yarn.

To order any of the kits in this book, or to receive information about Claire Murray's finished hand-hooked rugs and other fine home accessories, please call or write: Claire Murray Designs, 867 Main Street, Osterville, MA 02655. Phone: 1-800-345-KITS.

CREDITS

Excerpts from "Messages From My Garden," *Outdoors and In* by Joshua Freeman Crowell, The Four Seas Company, 1920.

Excerpts from *An Island Patchwork*, Copyright 1941, and (c) renewed 1969 by Eleanor Early. Reprinted by permission of Houghton Mifflin Company. All rights reserved.

Excerpts from "My Home," by L. Eugene Eldridge, *Cape Cod Magazine*, 1921.

"Nantucket" and excerpts from "Brant Point Light" by William Wells Jordan, *Nantucket and Other Verse*, Haverford, PA, 1930.

Excerpts from *The Nantucket Scrap Basket*. Copyright, 1916, by William F. Macy and Roland B. Hussey. Copyright, 1930, by William F. Macy. Reprinted by permission of Houghton Mifflin Company. All rights reserved.

"Old Fashioned Garden," by Cole Porter. © 1919 Warner Bros. Inc. (renewed) All rights reserved. Used by permission.

Excerpts from "Neptune's Palace" and "Neptune's Vow" by T.N. Stone, M.D., *Cape Cod Rhymes*, Riverside Press, 1869.

Excerpt from "Advice to a Prophet" in *Advice To A Prophet And Other Poems*, copyright © 1959 and renewed 1987 by Richard Wilbur, reprinted by permission of Harcourt Brace & Company.

We have made every effort to credit the authors of the verses used throughout the book. We would appreciate any information on omissions for subsequent printings.

*Oil painting of Claire Murray in her Nantucket gardens
by Peter Quidley*

Special thanks to Nantucket Islanders for allowing us to

photograph their breathtaking gardens and homes, especially Siasconset residents

whose cascading roses and seaside cottages provided the perfect setting

for Claire Murray's Nantucket Inspirations.